❧ THE ❧
ULTIMATE
DINOSAUR
FIELD GUIDE

THE ULTIMATE DINOSAUR FIELD GUIDE

APPLESAUCE PRESS

MY FIELD NOTES

Every good scientist needs a field guide. It's an essential tool for identifying wildlife and telling one species apart from another. Field guides are best used out in the wild to learn about nature on the go while hiking or exploring. The pictures and descriptors make it easier to know what you're looking at. And there are field guides for just about everything, including all kinds of plants and animals. You can make your own field guides or add onto field guides just by taking notes about what you see when you look at different wildlife. What color is it? How big is it? Where did you find it? Knowing those details will help you recognize it when you see it again!

There are about 700 different types of true dinosaurs, which are a family of reptiles that lived millions of years ago. And there are also hundreds of species of other prehistoric creatures from early mammals like horses and elephants to early whales and sharks. This field guide will tell you about a few of the biggest, best, most recognizable species you might have encountered if you were out in the jungle in prehistoric times.

Of course, these days you can't see live dinosaurs out in the wild. They all went extinct millions of years ago during a mass extinction event at the end of the Cretaceous period. Some prehistoric animals evolved into different species that you can still see today, and some species died out. Most of what we know about dinosaurs comes from fossilized bones and even fossilized imprints and footprints showing evidence of different species. Scientists have used that evidence to recreate what dinosaurs would have looked like and to come up with theories about where and how they lived.

Even though there aren't live dinosaurs roaming around in the wild, that doesn't mean you can't identify dinos in your everyday life—they're visible everywhere. Next time you're watching a dinosaur movie or going to a museum, take out your trusty field guide to help you identify the different species. You might even see dinosaurs on toys or clothes that you can identify! And as you dig more into the land of dinos and see new species, keep your own notes and records about what you learn so you can become a true dino expert.

DIMETRODON LIMBATUS

(CARNIVORE)

PERMIAN PERIOD

TALL SAIL ON ITS BACK

Huge spines running down its back support a sail made of skin. *Dimetrodon* is the first known species with a sail.

**6 FEET TALL
(1.8 METERS)**

**WEIGHS UP TO 550 POUNDS
(250 KILOGRAMS)**

**15 FEET LONG
(4.6 METERS)**

Serrated, saw-like teeth are a must-have for carnivores. The sharp edges help them chomp down on prey.

SERRATED TEETH

↓

SQUAT BODY THAT WALKS ON ALL FOUR LEGS

↑

Dimetrodon is warm-blooded, which means it isn't a true dinosaur. It's actually a protomammal, but it reproduces by laying eggs.

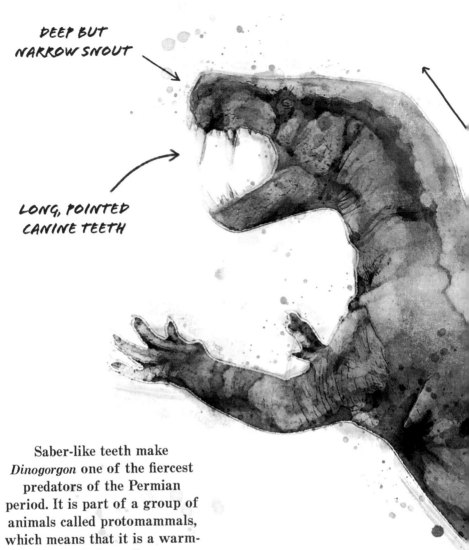

DEEP BUT NARROW SNOUT

LONG, POINTED CANINE TEETH

Saber-like teeth make *Dinogorgon* one of the fiercest predators of the Permian period. It is part of a group of animals called protomammals, which means that it is a warm-blooded reptile.

LEGS UPRIGHT AND CLOSE TO THE MIDDLE OF THE BODY

The leg shape and placement allows for quick movement. It runs on all fours when hunting prey.

DINOGORGON RUBIDGEI

(CARNIVORE)

PERMIAN PERIOD

6 FEET LONG
(1.8 METERS)

ABOUT 2 FEET TALL
(0.6 METERS)

TITANOSUCHUS FEROX

(CARNIVORE)

PERMIAN PERIOD

9 FEET LONG
(2.74 METERS)

SMOOTH SKIN

Unlike the scaly skin typical of reptiles, *Titanosuchus* has smooth skin partly covered in hair.

LONG SKULL

SHARP INCISORS AND FANG-LIKE CANINE TEETH

Size isn't *Titanosuchus'* only advantage as a hunter. Its pointed teeth make it a fierce predator, chomping down on prey easily.

WALKS ON ALL FOURS ON SHORT LEGS

Titanosuchus has a very similar body shape to crocodiles. The name "suchus" is actually shared by the West African crocodile, which has the scientific name *Crocodylus suchus*.

Moschops is named for its unique head shape.
Moschops comes from the Greek for "calf face."

DOMED HEAD

Moschops moves on all fours,
but unlike other creatures
that are low to the ground,
Moschops has a unique elbow
joint that allows it to walk
upright more than crawl.

JOINTED ELBOWS

5 FEET TALL
(1.5 METERS)

9 FEET LONG
(2.74 METERS)

This herbivore isn't a predator, but it does fight by butting heads, which may be the reason for its short, thick skull. The domed head is reinforced with thick, dense bone.

The hippopotamus-like *Moschops* lives partly on land and partly in water.

HEAVY-BUILT BODY
AND SHORT NECK

MOSCHOPS CAPENSIS

(HERBIVORE)

PERMIAN PERIOD

JONKERIA
TRUCULENTA

(OMNIVORE)

PERMIAN PERIOD

3-5 FEET TALL
(0.9-1.5 METERS)

12-16 FEET LONG
(3.65-4.9 METERS)

The head shape of *Jonkeria* is similar to *Titanosuchus*, but what sets these two apart is their body shape. *Jonkeria* has much shorter limbs and a bulkier body than *Titanosuchus*. The two live in the same habitat and likely cross paths with one another.

SNOUT THAT IS TWICE AS LONG AS IT IS WIDE

LARGE INCISOR AND CANINE TEETH

Jonkeria is both a meat eater and a plant eater, but it's not always a hunter. Its large body makes it very intimidating. If it comes across smaller predators who have caught prey, *Jonkeria* will scare off the smaller predator and steal its meal.

SHORT LIMBS AND BULKY BODY

ARCHOSAURUS ROSSICUS

(CARNIVORE)

PERMIAN PERIOD

HUNTS ON ALL FOURS

10 FEET LONG
(3 METERS)

SKULL MEASURES OVER 1 FOOT LONG (0.3 METERS)

The downward-kinked snout gives *Archosaurus* a snaggle-toothed look.

SNOUT THAT POINTS DOWN AT THE END

LONG, SHARP TEETH

Even though that hooked jaw shape looks a little silly, it has a purpose. The shape helps *Archosaurus* hold onto its prey.

SMILOSUCHUS GREGORII

(CARNIVORE)

TRIASSIC PERIOD

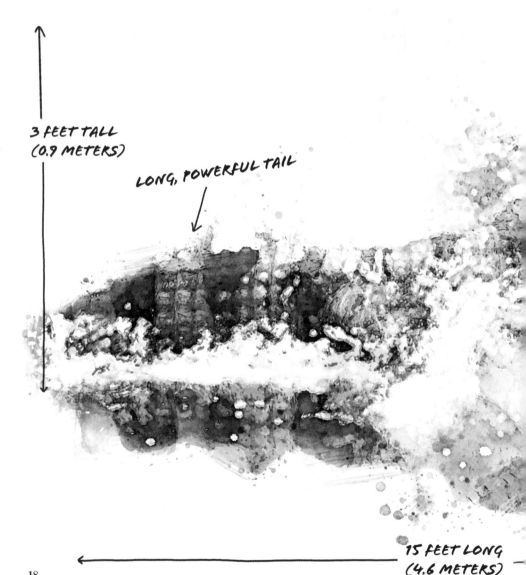

3 FEET TALL
(0.9 METERS)

LONG, POWERFUL TAIL

15 FEET LONG
(4.6 METERS)

Smilosuchus is part of a family called phytosaurs that look a lot like crocodiles. The big difference between *Smilosuchus* and a croc is the placement of the nostrils. Crocodiles have nostrils at the front of the snout, but *Smilosuchus* has nostrils closer to the eyes.

NOSTRILS FAR BACK ON ITS SNOUT NEAR ITS EYES

LARGE, BLADELIKE TEETH

Smilosuchus has teeth that are positioned at the back of the mouth to help it easily slice into prey.

WALKS ON ALL FOURS ON SHORT LIMBS

This dangerous carnivore is comfortable both in the water and on land, much like a crocodile. It hunts larger creatures like *Placerias hesternus*.

Smaller specimens can be as small as half the size of the *Herrerasaurus* noted here.

LONG, NARROW SKULL FILLED WITH DOZENS OF TEETH

WEIGHS UP TO 700 POUNDS (318 KILOGRAMS)

SHORT ARMS ABOUT HALF THE SIZE OF THE LEGS

Each arm has five fingers, but *Herrerasaurus* really only uses three fingers for catching prey.

HERRERASAURUS ISCHIGUALASTENSIS

(CARNIVORE)

TRIASSIC PERIOD

This thick back tail helps *Herrerasaurus* balance out all of its weight while it stands.

LONG, THICK BACK TAIL

STRONG LEGS AND LONG FEET WITH FIVE TOES

5 FEET TALL
(1.5 METERS)

Herrerasaurus has five toes, but only the three middle toes are useful in bearing its weight. With those strong back legs, *Herrerasaurus* is entirely bipedal, which means it walks on two legs, and it's a pretty fast runner.

20 FEET LONG
(6 METERS)

EODROMAEUS MURPHI

(CARNIVORE)

TRIASSIC PERIOD

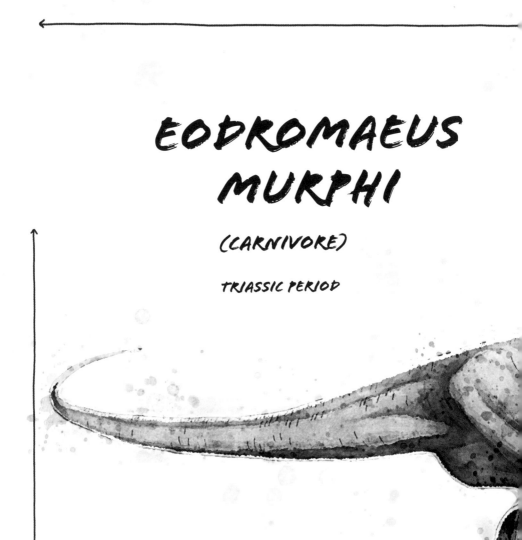

1-2 FEET TALL
(0.3-0.6 METERS)

Because of its strong back
legs, *Eodromaeus* walks
upright on two legs rather
than on all fours.

WEIGHS 10-15 POUNDS
(4.5-6.8 KILOGRAMS)

LOW, RECTANGULAR SKULL

SHARP TEETH

Eodromaeus is a carnivore that uses its fingers, teeth, and speed to catch prey.

SHORT ARMS AND LONGER HIND LEGS

Its arms have grasping fingers: three that are frequently used and two that are less often used.

Coelophysis has excellent vision and great depth perception, which are very useful traits in a hunter.

SLENDER NECK AND LONG, NARROW HEAD

LONG, NARROW JAW

Coelophysis has a jaw with plenty of bladelike, sharp, serrated teeth to help it catch prey.

3 FEET TALL (0.9 METERS)

ARMS WITH FOUR GRASPING CLAWS

Only three of Coelophysis' grasping claws are functional. The fourth is much smaller and not helpful in catching prey.

COELOPHYSIS BAURI

(CARNIVORE)

TRIASSIC PERIOD

← FAST, BIPEDAL RUNNER

**WEIGHS ABOUT 50 POUNDS
(22.7 KILOGRAMS)**

Hollow bones give it its light weight
and make it a quick, agile hunter.

6-9 FEET LONG
(1.8-2.74 METERS)

The name *Placerias* actually means "broad body." Its body looks somewhat similar to a hippopotamus. *Placerias* is able to submerge itself in water

HUSKY, BARREL-SHAPED BODY

WEIGHS UP TO 2,000 POUNDS
(907 KILOGRAMS)

5 FEET TALL
(1.5 METERS)

SHORT, SQUAT LEGS

Placerias walks on all fours and travels in herds to protect itself from predators.

11 FEET LONG
(3.35 METERS)

PLACERIAS HESTERNUS

(HERBIVORE)

POWERFUL NECK

TRIASSIC PERIOD

BEAK-LIKE SNOUT AND SHORT TUSKS

Despite the tusks, *Placerias* is an herbivore. It eats grass near lakes and rivers.

Placerias is a member of a protomammal group called dicynodonts, which share the same beak-like snout.

PLATEOSAURUS ENGELHARDTI

(HERBIVORE)

TRIASSIC PERIOD

WEIGHS 1,300-8,800 POUNDS (590-3,990 KILOGRAMS)

Because of its heavy size, *Plateosaurus* is prone to getting stuck in especially muddy areas.

POWERFUL HIND LEGS

Plateosaurus is bipedal, walking on two legs. Because of the shape of its feet, *Plateosaurus* walks around on its toes.

16-33 FEET LONG (4.87-10 METERS)

SMALL
SKULL

FLEXIBLE
NECK

It has a long neck with 10
vertebrae, which allows it to
be flexible, and its tail has
at least 40 vertebrae, which
allows it to be mobile.

9-10 FEET TALL
(2.74-3 METERS)

MUSCULAR ARMS WITH
SHORT, SHARP CLAWS

Its claws are used both
for grasping food and
for defending against
predators.

The first part of this dinosaur's name, *Thecodontosaurus*, means "socket-tooth lizard." The name is a reference to the shape of its teeth. Based on that tooth shape, *Thecodontosaurus* is likely an herbivore or omnivore.

LARGE SKULL AND LEAF-SHAPED TEETH

ARMS MUCH SHORTER THAN ITS LEGS

Thecodontosaurus is bipedal and has five fingers on each hand.

THECODONTOSAURUS ANTIQUUS

(HERBIVORE/OMNIVORE)

TRIASSIC PERIOD

LONG TAIL COMPARED TO BODY

Thecodontosaurus has an exceptionally long tail that can be longer than its head, neck, and body length put together.

1-2 FEET TALL (0.3-0.6 METERS)

WEIGHS ABOUT 25 POUNDS (11.3 KILOGRAMS)

4-6 FEET LONG (1.2-1.8 METERS)

ALLOSAURUS FRAGILIS

(CARNIVORE)

JURASSIC PERIOD

POWERFUL BACK LEGS

Allosaurus feeds a lot like falcons do, pinning carcasses with its feet and ripping off chunks of flesh with powerful jerks of its neck.

30 FEET LONG
(9.14 METERS)

LIGHT, SLENDER SKULL

Allosaurus horns aren't used for fighting. They're used for attracting mates or recognizing other *Allosaurus*.

SHORT HORNS OVER ITS EYES

SERRATED TEETH UP TO 3 INCHES LONG (7.6 CENTIMETERS)

STRONG ARMS WITH LARGE, THREE-CLAWED HANDS

Its claws have a hooked shape useful for grabbing onto prey. *Allosaurus* hunts in packs to gang up on prey (or fights over the same prey).

15-16 FEET TALL (4.6-4.9 METERS)

WEIGHS 1,500-2,200 POUNDS (680-1,000 KILOGRAMS)

THIN, PAIRED CRESTS
ON TOP OF ITS HEAD

The crests aren't useful in combat, but they may be used in choosing a mate or identifying other *Dilophosaurus*.

SHARP BACK TEETH

Dilophosaurus loses its teeth and replaces them with new, healthier teeth.

WEAK JAW

Dilophosaurus doesn't have much power in its bite, so it relies on its arms, legs, and teeth to catch prey.

POWERFUL ARMS
WITH FOUR FINGERS
(THE FOURTH ISN'T
FUNCTIONAL)

23 FEET LONG
(7 METERS)

DILOPHOSAURUS WETHERILLI

(CARNIVORE)

JURASSIC PERIOD

Compared to other dinosaurs, *Dilophosaurus* is medium-sized. It is about the size of a brown bear.

SLENDER, MEDIUM-SIZED BODY

**6 FEET TALL
(1.8 METERS)**

**WEIGHS ABOUT 880 POUNDS
(400 KILOGRAMS)**

CRYOLOPHOSAURUS ELLIOTI

(CARNIVORE)

JURASSIC PERIOD

8 FEET TALL
(2.43 METERS)

Cryolophosaurus lives in lush forests.

The fragile crest has a somewhat comb-like appearance and is actually made from an extension of the skull bones fused onto horns coming up near the eye sockets.

DEEP SKULL

BONY, RIDGED CREST ATOP THE HEAD

Its bony pompadour has earned *Cryolophosaurus* the nickname "Elvisaurus" thanks to the resemblance between its crest and his signature hairdo.

THREE-CLAWED HANDS

WEIGHS AROUND 1,000 POUNDS (450 KILOGRAMS)

21 FEET LONG (6.4 METERS)

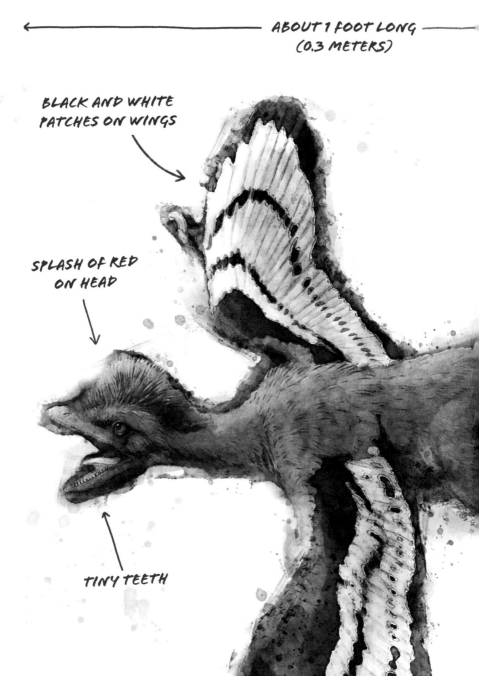

BLACK AND WHITE
PATCHES ON WINGS

SPLASH OF RED
ON HEAD

TINY TEETH

FEATHERED BODY

Anchiornis has dinofuzz
(the prehistoric precursor
to feathers).

ABOUT ½ FOOT TALL
(0.15 METERS)

Long legs usually make
for a good runner, but
the feathers covering
its legs make *Anchiornis*
slower than you'd expect.

LONG ARMS AND LEGS

ANCHIORNIS HUXLEYI

(CARNIVORE)

JURASSIC PERIOD

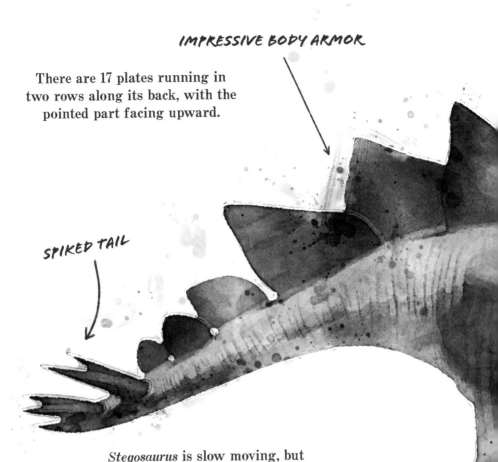

IMPRESSIVE BODY ARMOR

There are 17 plates running in two rows along its back, with the pointed part facing upward.

SPIKED TAIL

Stegosaurus is slow moving, but its spiked tail is good defense against attacking predators.

STEGOSAURUS STENOPS

(HERBIVORE)

JURASSIC PERIOD

30 FEET LONG
(9.14 METERS)

WEIGHS UP TO 7 TONS

14-17 FEET TALL
(4.26-5.18 METERS)

Stegosaurus is part of the Thyreophora—a group dinosaurs
known for having body armor—like *Ankylosaurus*.

Apatosaurus has unusually shaped bones that almost make it look aquatic.

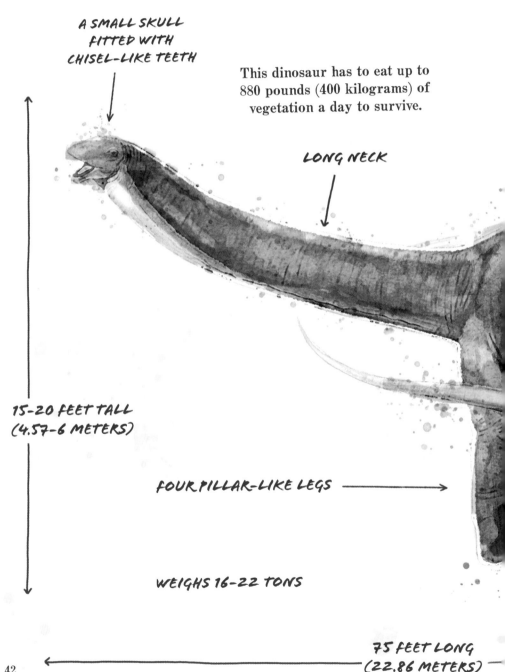

A SMALL SKULL FITTED WITH CHISEL-LIKE TEETH

This dinosaur has to eat up to 880 pounds (400 kilograms) of vegetation a day to survive.

LONG NECK

15-20 FEET TALL (4.57-6 METERS)

FOUR PILLAR-LIKE LEGS ⟶

WEIGHS 16-22 TONS

75 FEET LONG (22.86 METERS)

APATOSAURUS AJAX

(HERBIVORE)

JURASSIC PERIOD

Apatosaurus is a member of the sauropod family along with *Brontosaurus, Diplodocus, Camarasaurus,* and *Brachiosaurus.* They all share a similar body shape, but have subtle differences in size.

BULKY BODY

LONG, WHIPLIKE TAIL

CAMARASAURUS SUPREMUS

(HERBIVORE)

JURASSIC PERIOD

Camarasaurus eats tougher vegetation than other sauropods.

WEIGHS UP TO 47 TONS

Camarasaurus has the classic long neck of the sauropod family. The long sauropod necks have a unique structure with hollow chambers between the vertebrae, helping the bones in their neck be both strong and light.

LONG NECK

BLUNT SNOUT AND ARCHED HEAD MAKE THE SKULL LOOK SQUARE

30 FEET TALL (9.14 METERS)

SHORTER FRONT LEGS THAN BACK LEGS

Its shoulder blades are low and its hips are high. This allows its legs to somewhat line up even though they aren't the same length.

Brachiosaurus feeds on coniferous trees, gingkoes, and cycads. It can eat 880 pounds (400 kilograms) of vegetation a day.

HAS A WIDE, THICK JAW FILLED WITH SPOON-LIKE TEETH THAT IT USES TO STRIP LEAVES OFF BRANCHES

USES ITS LONG NECK TO REACH LEAVES HIGH UP IN TREES

LONGER FRONT LEGS THAN BACK LEGS—DIFFERENT FROM OTHER SAUROPOD DINOSAURS

BRACHIOSAURUS ALTITHORAX

(HERBIVORE)

JURASSIC PERIOD

Brachiosaurus travels in herds, moving to a new place once the old one runs out of vegetation—that much eating quickly strips trees bare.

40 FEET TALL
(12.2 METERS)

WEIGHS UP TO 62 TONS

47

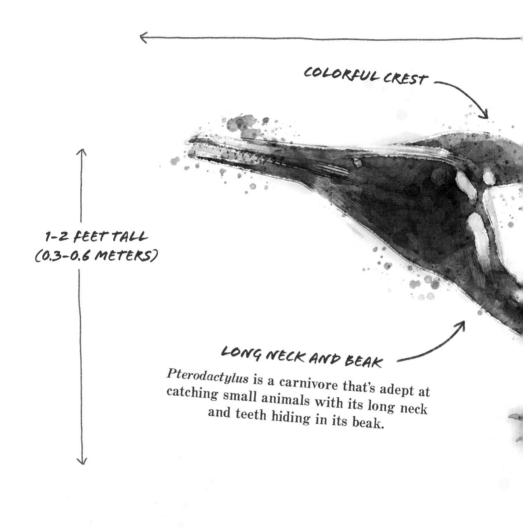

COLORFUL CREST

1-2 FEET TALL
(0.3-0.6 METERS)

LONG NECK AND BEAK

Pterodactylus is a carnivore that's adept at catching small animals with its long neck and teeth hiding in its beak.

WEIGHS UP TO 10 POUNDS
(4.5 KILOGRAMS)

PTERODACTYLUS ANTIQUUS

(CARNIVORE)

JURASSIC PERIOD

WINGSPAN 3 FEET WIDE
(0.9 METERS)

BIRD-LIKE BODY

"Pterodactyl" is the common name
for a group of winged reptiles
called pterosaurs. *Pterodactylus* is
just one of 130 different members
in this family.

LARGE WINGS

The wings stretch out over its
elongated fourth finger—the
name *Pterodactylus* even means
"winged finger."

MOUTH FULL OF
SHARP TEETH

Despite the teeth, *Velociraptor* more often swallows its food whole, just using its teeth to tear off large chunks.

2-3 FEET TALL
(0.6-0.9 METERS)

STRONG ARMS WITH
GRASPING HANDS AND
SHARP CLAWS

EXTENDABLE TOE ON EACH FOOT
TIPPED WITH A LARGE CLAW

The claw is used to tackle
and trap its prey. While
it walks, the claw points
upright. When it attacks, the
claw snaps downward.

VELOCIRAPTOR MONGOLIENSIS

(CARNIVORE)

CRETACEOUS PERIOD

STIFF TAIL USED FOR BALANCE

FEATHERS ON THE BODY

The feathers help keep nests of eggs
warm before they hatch.

Velociraptor can't fly, but it is similar
to birds in other ways—it is somewhat
warm-blooded and has a wishbone.

WEIGHS AROUND 60 POUNDS
(27 KILOGRAMS)

7 FEET LONG
(2.1 METERS)

DSUNGARIPTERUS WEII

(CARNIVORE)

CRETACEOUS PERIOD

The body size and shape indicate that it spends more time on land than in the air since it's not very aerodynamic.

STURDY, STOUT BODY COVERED IN A COAT OF INSULATING FUZZ

4 FEET TALL (1.2 METERS)

WINGS EXTENDING OVER AN EXTREMELY LONG FOURTH FINGER

BONY CREST RUNNING DOWN THE TOP OF THE SKULL

← UPTURNED, TOOTHY BEAK

Dsungaripterus has flat, crushing teeth at the back of the jaw. The combination of pointed beak and teeth in the back help *Dsungaripterus* crack the shells of invertebrates, like ammonites.

LARGE HEAD AND NECK

Compared to the size of its body, the head and neck of *Dsungaripterus* are very large, coming in at around 3 feet long (0.9 meters).

WEIGHS ABOUT 30 POUNDS (13.6 KILOGRAMS)

WINGSPAN 10 FEET WIDE (3 METERS) ⟶

LONG FLIGHT FEATHERS ON THE ARMS, LEGS, AND AT THE END OF THE TAIL

The asymmetrical shape of the feathers help *Microraptor* fly. They are not just for warmth or display.

WEIGHS ABOUT 2 POUNDS (0.9 KILOGRAMS)

Small but populous, *Microraptor* is a common dinosaur in its habitat.

FOUR WING-LIKE LIMBS

The groups of feathers on its arms and legs give *Microraptor* four separate wings. Although it can't fly long distances, it can glide over shorter distances with its limbs extended out to the side.

MICROKAPTOR GUI

(CARNIVORE)

CRETACEOUS PERIOD

THICK COVERING OF FEATHERS

1 FOOT TALL (0.3 METERS)

2-3 FEET LONG (0.6-0.9 METERS)

SUCHOMIMUS TENERENSIS

(CARNIVORE)

CRETACEOUS PERIOD

LOW SAIL ALONG THE BACK →

Enlarged spines running down its back hold up the humped sail.

8-9 FEET TALL
(2.43-2.74 METERS)

WEIGHS 3-5 TONS

Suchomimus is a "crocodile mimic" in the shape
of its skull with a long snout and lower jaw.

CROCODILE-LIKE SNOUT

100 THIN TEETH
The teeth are slightly curved,
somewhat like a fishing hook,
and are adept at catching
slippery prey like fish.

THICK, GRASPING CLAWS
Suchomimus hunts both on land and in
water, using the effective combination of
claws and teeth to catch small prey or
scavenge for dead animals.

30 FEET LONG
(9.14 METERS)

Tall spines hold up a large sail running down its neck, back, and tail. Each spine can be up to 1 foot tall (0.3 meters).

HIGH, PROMINENT RIDGE RUNNING ALONG THE BACK

10 FEET TALL (3 METERS)

WEIGHS 3-5 TONS

Despite its massive size, *Acrocanthosaurus* walks upright on two feet rather than on all fours.

40 FEET LONG (12 METERS)

Acrocanthosaurus is a carnivore that uses its large claws to dig into its prey. It holds its prey close while delivering a final bite.

← THREE-CLAWED ARMS

ACROCANTHOSAURUS ATOKENSIS

(CARNIVORE)

CRETACEOUS PERIOD

Each spine can grow up to 7 feet tall (2.1 meters). *Spinosaurus* has flexible vertebrae and can arch its back to spread its sail. The sail is brightly colored.

LARGE SPINE AND SKIN-LIKE SAIL ALONG THE BACK

DENSE BONES

Its bone density acts like a ballast to help keep it submerged in the water when it hunts in lakes or rivers.

15 FEET TALL (4.6 METERS)

WIDE, CLAWED FEET

40 FEET LONG (12.2 METERS)

SPINOSAURUS AEGYPTIACUS

(CARNIVORE)

CRETACEOUS PERIOD

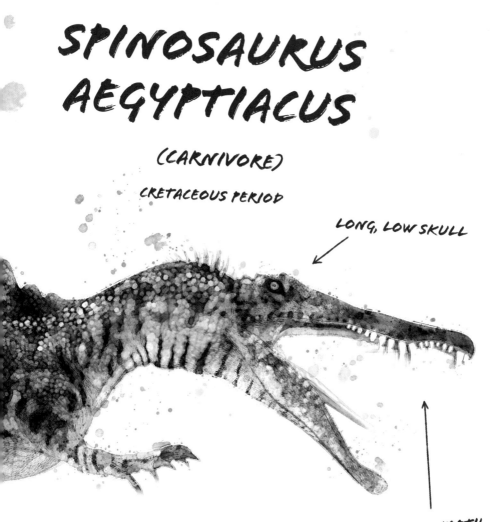

LONG, LOW SKULL

CONICAL TEETH

SHORT HIND LIMBS

The size and shape of the limbs is similar to that of prehistoric whales and other water-dwelling animals. Its wide feet help *Spinosaurus* paddle in the water, and its weight is shifted slightly forward; this helps it swim and walk on all fours when it's on land.

WEIGHS 7-9 TONS

GIGANOTOSAURUS CAROLINII

(CARNIVORE)

CRETACEOUS PERIOD

THIN, POINTED TAIL

Despite its large size, *Giganotosaurus* is fairly agile. This bipedal dinosaur uses its tail for balance and to make quick turns while it runs. It can reach speeds of up to 30 miles per hour.

WEIGHS 6-8 TONS

Its skull alone measures up to 5 feet long (1.5 meters).

LONG, DEEP SKULL

RIDGED CREST

FLATTENED, SERRATED TEETH

The sharp, shark-like tooth shape is a common trait for all members of the dinosaur family Carcharodontosauridae, which has some of the biggest, fiercest predators to rival even the tyrannosaurs.

THREE CLAWED FINGERS ON EACH ARM

12 FEET TALL (3.65 METERS)

The ridge differs in color from the rest of the body and is likely not used for anything other than display.

ROUGH RIDGE OF BONE ON THE BROW

KNIFE-SHAPED TEETH USED TO RIP APART PREY

Eocarcharia translates to "dawn shark," a reference to its serrated, slicing teeth that are as powerful as a shark's.

It's part of the family Carcharodontosauridae, which is known for having these distinctive, shark-like teeth.

6 FEET TALL
(3.65 METERS)

WEIGHS 1-2 TONS

25 FEET LONG
(7.6 METERS)

EOCARCHARIA DINOPS

(CARNIVORE)

LONG, DEEP SKULL

CRETACEOUS PERIOD

SAUROPOSEIDON PROTELES

(HERBIVORE)

CRETACEOUS PERIOD

Sauroposeidon is the
tallest known dinosaur.

WEIGHS 45-65 TONS

Sauroposeidon uses its long neck to reach vegetation high up in trees.

LONG NECK

Even compared to other members of the sauropod family, *Sauroposeidon* has an incredibly long neck.

WALKS ON ALL FOURS

Although it walks on all fours like other sauropods, if *Sauroposeidon* stood up straight it would be over 56 feet tall (17 meters).

20-23 FEET TALL (6-7 METERS)

89-112 FEET LONG (27-34 METERS)

SMALL SKULL AND TOOTHLESS JAWS

The toothless *Linhenykus* is the dinosaur equivalent of an anteater. It eats using its stocky forearms and claws to dig for insects.

SINGLE CLAWED FINGER ON EACH HAND

2 FEET TALL (0.6 METERS)

SHORT, STUBBY ARMS

Linhenykus is part of a family called alvarezsaurs that rely heavily on one claw. While other alvarezsaurs have non-functional second or third fingers, *Linhenykus* truly only has one finger.

WEIGHS 5-10 POUNDS (2.3-4.5 KILOGRAMS)

LINHENYKUS MONODACTYLUS

(CARNIVORE)

CRETACEOUS PERIOD

OVIRAPTOR PHILOCERATOPS

(CARNIVORE)

CRETACEOUS PERIOD

COVERED IN FEATHERS

Oviraptor lays nests of eggs and sits on top of them to keep them warm—a behavior called brooding.

BIPEDAL

5 FEET LONG
(1.5 METERS)

CREST ON TOP OF HEAD

**TOOTHLESS,
PARROT-LIKE BEAK**

The curved upper jaw allows
Oviraptor to easily crush eggs or
shellfish. Some bones jutting down
from the roof of its mouth help it
crush small morsels, but *Oviraptor*
swallows most mouthfuls whole.

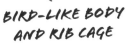

**BIRD-LIKE BODY
AND RIB CAGE**

**3 FEET TALL
(0.9 METERS)**

**WEIGHS 55 POUNDS
(25 KILOGRAMS)**

The eye position gives *Troodon* binocular vision, and its brain measures about five times larger than expected for a dinosaur of its size, making *Troodon* a clever hunter that's quickly able to pinpoint small, scurrying prey.

LARGE, FORWARD-FACING EYES

ARMS WITH THREE GRASPING FINGERS

SMALL TEETH
The curved, serrated teeth are small but powerful.

8 FEET LONG
(2.43 METERS)

TROODON FORMOSUS

(OMNIVORE)

CRETACEOUS PERIOD

WEIGHS ABOUT 100 POUNDS
(45 KILOGRAMS)

Like other members of the raptor family, *Troodon* is covered in feathers.

3 FEET TALL (0.9 METERS)

← EXTENDABLE CLAW ON EACH FOOT

Troodon is a bipedal dinosaur that's known for being a fast runner.

GORGOSAURUS LIBRATUS

(CARNIVORE)

CRETACEOUS PERIOD

8-12
FEET TALL
(2.43-3.65
METERS)

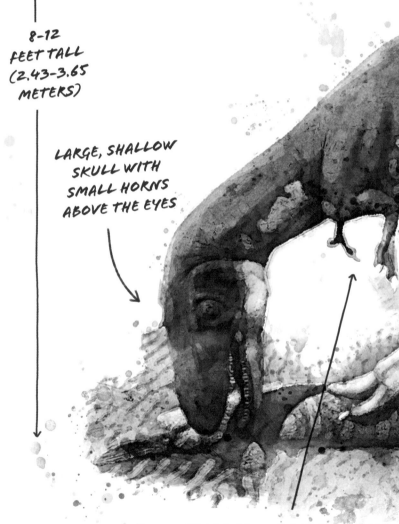

LARGE, SHALLOW
SKULL WITH
SMALL HORNS
ABOVE THE EYES

SHORT FRONT LIMBS WITH
TWO GRASPING FINGERS

WEIGHS 3 TONS

As it grows, a young *Gorgosaurus* can gain over 110 pounds (50 kilograms) each year.

Gorgosaurus is an apex predator.

LIGHT BUILD AND LONG, POWERFUL LEGS

The agile *Gorgosaurus* is a member of the tyrannosaur family. Compared to other tyrannosaurids, *Gorgosaurus* is lean.

It's a fast runner that's both a hunter and scavenger. It has an excellent sense of smell that aids it in sniffing out both live prey and carcasses.

30 FEET LONG (9.14 METERS)

WEIGHS ABOUT 2-3 TONS

Carnotaurus can move quickly from side to side, which is very useful for hunting while running.

Rival individuals combat each other by ramming their heads together.

FLAT SKULL WITH THIN SIDES

SHORT, TRIANGULAR HORN PROJECTING OVER EACH EYE

POWERFUL JAW WITH WIDE, BLUNT TEETH

The combination of a strong jaw and blunt teeth helps *Carnotaurus* easily kill prey and chomp directly through bone.

SHORT ARMS WITH FOUR FINGERS

Only three out of the four fingers have claws, and only two of those fingers have bones.

CARNOTAURUS SASTREI

(CARNIVORE)

CRETACEOUS PERIOD

SCALY SKIN WITH ROWS OF
FLATTENED BUMPS

8 FEET TALL
(2.43 METERS)

POWERFUL BACK LEGS

Carnotaurus is a bipedal dinosaur
that can reach speeds of up to
40 miles per hour.

30 FEET LONG
(9.14 METERS)

Masiakasaurus is part of the theropod family, which typically has downward-pointing teeth. The hooked shape of its teeth is perfect for a more diverse diet, including latching onto fish or eating some fruit.

FORWARD-PROJECTING TEETH

STIFF NECK AND RIBS

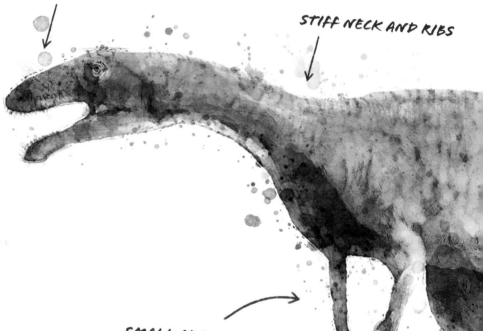

SMALL ARMS AND GRASPING HANDS

Like other raptor dinosaurs, *Masiakasaurus* is bipedal and uses its clawed fingers to grab prey. It has four fingers with the middle two being the longest and most agile.

MASIAKASAURUS KNOPFLERI

(OMNIVORE)

CRETACEOUS PERIOD

REACHES ADULT SIZE
AROUND AGE 10

1-2 FEET TALL
(0.3-0.6 METERS)

WEIGHS ABOUT 80 POUNDS
(36 KILOGRAMS)

7 FEET LONG
(2.13 METERS)

ALBERTOSAURUS SARCOPHAGUS

(CARNIVORE)

CRETACEOUS PERIOD

LONG TAIL TO
BALANCE OUT THE
HEAD AND BODY

SCALY SKIN

11 FEET TALL
(3.35 METERS)

POWERFUL HIND LEGS
WITH FOUR TOES

WEIGHS 2 TONS

30 FEET LONG
(9.14 METERS)

Albertosaurus is smaller and more agile than many of its tyrannosaur relatives.

LARGE, SLEEK BODY

Albertosaurus has colored horns over its eyes, likely used to identify other Albertosaurus or for mating.

BIG SKULL

LARGE, SAW-LIKE TEETH

Albertosaurus teeth excel at tearing off flesh, but they aren't very useful for chewing. Instead, Albertosaurus swallows large chunks of its prey whole.

SHORT ARMS WITH TWO FINGERS

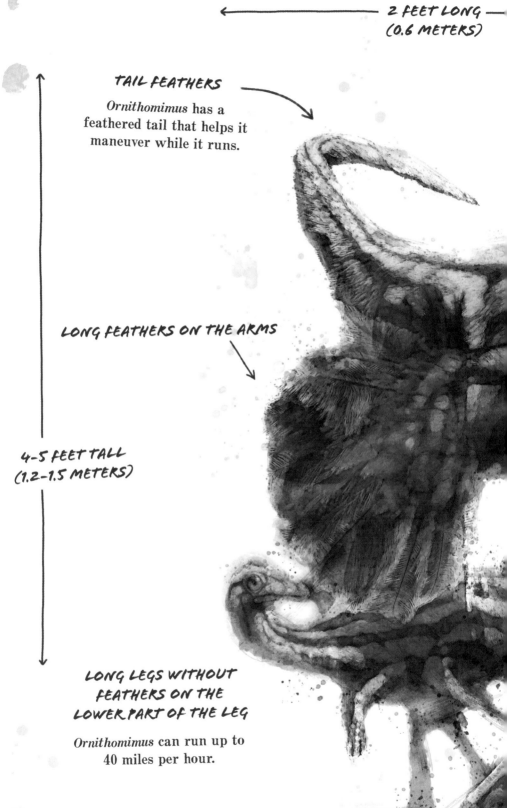

2 FEET LONG
(0.6 METERS)

TAIL FEATHERS

Ornithomimus has a
feathered tail that helps it
maneuver while it runs.

LONG FEATHERS ON THE ARMS

4-5 FEET TALL
(1.2-1.5 METERS)

LONG LEGS WITHOUT
FEATHERS ON THE
LOWER PART OF THE LEG

Ornithomimus can run up to
40 miles per hour.

TOOTHLESS BEAK

GRACEFUL NECK

WEIGHS ABOUT 370 POUNDS (168 KILOGRAMS)

Ornithomimus eats both insects and small prey with a combination of its arms and beak. Its long arms and claws snatch small prey, pull down tree branches, and dig in the dirt.

LONG ARMS WITH LARGE CLAWS

ORNITHOMIMUS EDMONTICUS

(OMNIVORE)

CRETACEOUS PERIOD

LONG NECK AND TINY HEAD

WEIGHS 3-5 TONS

10-FOOT-LONG
ARMS (3 METERS)

3-FOOT-LONG CLAWS
(0.9 METERS)

Though intimidating, the claws
aren't especially sharp. This
omnivore uses them to gather
leaves into its mouth or dig into
mounds of termites.

THERIZINOSAURUS CHELONIFORMIS

(OMNIVORE)

CRETACEOUS PERIOD

16 FEET TALL
(4.9 METERS)

LARGE, SQUAT BODY

With its hefty body and four-toed feet, *Therizinosaurus* doesn't move very quickly.

FOUR-TOED FEET

33 FEET LONG
(10 METERS)

One of the biggest flying animals ever,
its wings are made up of skin stretched
between the body and extremely long
fourth fingers.

HEAD AND NECK
SIMILAR TO A STORK

Rather than flapping its wings
constantly, *Quetzalcoatlus* glides to
fly. It can travel up to 10,000 miles
(16,093 kilometers) at a time.

FEATHERED BODY

BODY SIMILAR
TO A BAT

SHARP, POINTED
BEAK

16 FEET TALL
(4.87 METERS)

LONG LEGS

Quetzalcoatlus is part of the
pterosaur family, like *Pterodactylus*,
and it is as comfortable hunting on
land as it is gliding in the air.

QUETZALCOATLUS NORTHROPI

(CARNIVORE)

CRETACEOUS PERIOD

440-550 POUNDS
(200-250 KILOGRAMS)

The horns and neck frill are used for protection, as *Triceratops* lives alongside fearsome predators like *Tyrannosaurus rex*. The horns are able to heal after attacks. Protection is especially important since *Triceratops* typically travels alone.

BONY NECK FRILL

THREE FACIAL HORNS

Triceratops is one of the most recognizable dinosaurs with its facical features.

WEIGHS 6-8 TONS

TRICERATOPS HORRIDUS

(HERBIVORE)

CRETACEOUS PERIOD

9-10 FEET TALL
(2.74-3 METERS)

HEAVY BODY AND
THICK LEGS

Triceratops is similar in shape to a rhinoceros. It carries its heavy body on all four legs.

29 FEET LONG
(8.8 METERS)

TYRANNOSAURUS REX

(CARNIVORE)

CRETACEOUS PERIOD

14 FEET TALL
(4.26 METERS)

WEIGHS 9 TONS

T. rex walks tilted forward on two powerful legs, somewhat parallel to the ground. Its massive tail counterbalances the weight of its head as it moves.

LARGE, DEEP SKULL

T. rex rams prey with serrated, spike-sized teeth with a force of more than 12,800 pounds (5,806 kilograms), easily puncturing flesh and bone. It swallows giant mouthfuls of flesh at a time.

Exceptionally strong neck and jaw muscles let *T. rex* kill its prey with a side-to-side shake of its head.

TINY, TWO-FINGERED ARMS

40 FEET LONG
(12.19 METERS)

Dorudon lives entirely in the water. The small size of its legs indicate they are not very useful for moving around on land.

SMALL LEGS AT THE SIDE OF THE BODY

WEIGHS 2 TONS

16 FEET LONG
(4.87 METERS)

Based on the jaw and tooth shape, *Dorudon* eats small marine animals. The teeth also give *Dorudon* its name, which means "spear-tooth."

POINTED, GRABBING TEETH AT THE FRONT OF THE JAW AND SHEARING TEETH IN THE CHEEK

LONG, NARROW SNOUT

LARGE HOLE IN THE LOWER JAW

The hole position is similar to holes that other whales have, and is likely used to help *Dorudon* hear while underwater.

DORUDON ATROX

(CARNIVORE)

CENOZOIC ERA

CARCHAROCLES MEGALODON

(CARNIVORE)

CENOZOIC ERA

NEWBORNS CAN BE
OVER 6 FEET LONG
(1.8 METERS) AT BIRTH

WEIGHS 65 TONS

Similar in body shape to the great white shark, this is the largest shark of all time. It prowls just about every prehistoric ocean preying on blubbery whales.

HUGE, FINELY SERRATED TEETH

The triangular shape of its teeth is similar to white sharks, but the size of its teeth is what's truly impressive. *Megalodon* teeth measure nearly 7 inches long (18 centimeters). A white shark's tooth is only about 2 inches (5 centimeters).

ABOUT APPLESAUCE PRESS BOOK PUBLISHERS

Good ideas ripen with time. From seed to harvest, Applesauce Press crafts books with beautiful designs, creative formats, and kid-friendly information on a variety of topics. Like our parent company, Cider Mill Press Book Publishers, our press bears fruit twice a year, publishing a new crop of titles each spring and fall.

"Where Good Books Are Ready for Press"

501 Nelson Place
Nashville, Tennessee 37214

cidermillpress.com